To; MY fellow Glover
Eagles

Why I Believe in Me

Always Believe
in you!,

Lauren

Class of 2016

What I Believe in Me

Why I Believe in Me

A Young Person's Guide to Mediating the Life of their Dreams

Lauren McGowen-Bond

AIM High Media & Publishing

AIM High Publishing

Why I Believe in Me: A Young Person's Guide to Mediating the Life of Their Dreams

By: Lauren McGowen-Bond
Author, Speaker, Certified Peer Mental Coach, Trained Peer Mediator

Published in the United States of America by:
AIM High Media & Publishing (Subsidiary of McLaughlin-Bond International)
4771 Sweetwater Blvd. #122
Sugar Land, TX 77479
www.AimHighPub.com

ISBN: 978-1-94296-201-4
Library of Congress Control: 2015954779

This title is also available on:
Kindle, Nook, iBooks, and as an AIM High Publishing eBook.
Visit www.AimHighPub.com/ebooks

Any internet addresses, (websites, blogs, etc.), and telephone numbers in this book are provided as a resource. They are not intended, in any way, to be or imply an endorsement by AIM High Media & Publishing, nor does AIM High Media & Publishing vouch for the content of these stated resources for the life of this book. All quotations used in this book are properly cited to give credit to the original author. Neither the author nor AIM High Media & Publishing intends to take credit for this material.

Editor: Tonoa Bond
Cover Photos: Jamicia Ware & Tonoa Bond
Cover Design: Ihor Tureha
Interior Design: AIM High Media & Publishing
Interior photos provided by Tonoa Bond, Jamicia Ware, Camille Caldwell & Denise Guess unless otherwise noted.

This book is dedicated to my mom for always supporting me and teaching me to believe in my dreams!

Also by Lauren McGowen-Bond

Why I Believe in Me: A Young Person's Guide to Mediating the Life of Their Dreams.

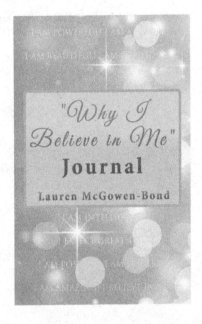

"Why I Believe in Me Journal. The workbook and journal accompaniment to this book.

ISBN #: 978-1-942962-05-2
Library of Congress Control #: 2015959519

Order Your Copy Today! www.ToKnowADream.com

For more information on how to continue your journey of self-belief go to www.ToKnowADream.com.

CONTENTS

FOREWORD

When Lauren was 5, she asked me why I was always writing. I explained to her I was an author and that I was writing a book to help others believe in themselves and their dreams. She then looked at me with determination and said, "I'm going to do that too." The very next weekend she finished her first fictional book titled, "The Princess and the Panda". And from that day forward, she simply never stopped writing.

Lauren has always had the mindset that she can accomplish anything she set her mind to. And for her, it does not matter if others believe she can be successful at whatever she is attempting. It also does not matter that she is attempting to accomplish things that are above her age level. All that matters is that she makes an effort knowing she can figure out the rest later.

She has always played the role of mediator for herself. She not only waited out every "no" she heard until she got the "yes" her Purpose deserved, but she also did the work necessary to ensure her dreams would come true. Lauren wanted to become a tri-athlete, and asked me every year, from first grade to fourth grade, if she could participate. I finally gave in and got her the swimming and biking lessons she needed to compete. For years, she asked to join a track club. When she did, she became a State and Junior Olympic qualified runner her first year.

Academically, Lauren excels in school. Artistically, she wows judges with her entries. And overall, she is simply extremely happy to be who she is called and Purposed to be. In one calendar year, her excellence was rewarded in two big ways: She was inducted into the National Elementary Honor Society and she received the President's Award for Educational

Foreword

Excellence. And she could not be prouder of having President Barack Obama's signature and two huge honors hanging on her wall of fame.

There are so many other examples of Lauren mediating for her dreams and never taking no for an answer. And every example leads to her truth and why she believes in her dreams. I would like to think she got that from me; and maybe a little of it she did. But in actuality, I truly believe she was born this way and that maybe she was sent to me so I could learn more from one who mastered it so early on. I am proud to say I could not have asked for a better guide.

It is my hope that the words Lauren shared throughout this book touch you in such a way that your belief in yourself and your dreams will forever be changed. That you will see yourself in a different light, and that you truly know that you can do whatever it is you put your mind to.

As Lauren has so aptly proved in her young, burgeoning career, age is nothing but a number and there is nothing a little persistence, faith in self, and dedication to purpose cannot conquer. Take a page out of Lauren's book and spend the rest of your life believing and knowing this one thing: That not only do you have a dream, but you ARE the dream. All you have to do is have the audacity to believe in it and you!

Keep Believing! Your power is waiting to be unleashed!

Tonoa Bond
MS, PhD(s), PCPsych, CPC
Mother, Lauren McGowen-Bond

INTRODUCTION

A Note from Lauren and the Publisher:

"I believe in me", while not grammatically correct, is a declaration that I make to remind myself and the world that I really do believe I can do whatever it is I put my mind to. This includes, 'write a book', which is why you are reading this book right now. However, I had to learn to mediate my fears and my faith to make this happen; and I figured if I could do it then you can do it too.

The word "Mediate" means to intervene in a dispute in order to bring about an agreement or reconciliation. Another definition says, 'to help make peace'. As you go after your dreams, you will find yourself stuck between fear and faith. Where, even though you have faith in your dreams, the fear you may feel about going after them will attempt to hold you back from following through. This is when mediation becomes necessary. You will need to intervene in your own internal dispute in your beliefs in order to shift your life from where you are to where you want to be. But you can do it! I believe in you!

In this book, I share with you mindset tools to help you learn to mediate your life and your dreams in varying situations. I hope that in using these tools you will learn to make peace with the things that are holding you back. I also hope that you realize you can do anything you set your mind to.

Each chapter in this book comes in four parts: The lesson, an affirmation statement, a Mediation Moment, and Words to Live By. In the lesson, I tell personal stories about a specific topic to encourage you to believe in yourself. Again, my goal is to let you know that if I could do it – get over my fear, mediate my beliefs, and follow my dreams – then you can do it too. The

Introduction

affirmation statement is to affirm you: to guide you to strongly state positive, life changing, things about yourself, as if a fact, to help you change your beliefs. The *Mediation Moments* offer tools and exercises to help you find agreement between the push and the pull in your belief system so you can end the struggle between fear and faith. And lastly, the '*Words to Live By*' are definitions of words that you need to know in order to be the most effective mediator you can be for yourself.

Sometimes, success requires you to need a little help in order to help yourself. Sometimes, you have to be willing to promise that you will believe in yourself no matter what. Therefore, on page 77, you will find your first Mediation Moment. It is a contract that you will make with yourself. This contract is a promise or vow that you will never give up on yourself during this journey and that you will keep moving forward until every dream you have made for yourself gets fulfilled. A contract also infers importance. So when you sign the contract, remember that you are important and that the most important thing you can do for yourself is to always believe in you.

Things will not change in your life unless you do the work to make them change. Therefore, this entire book is my mediation gift to you. Whether via a tip or an exercise, I have crafted every word to help you learn to mediate your dreams. Every exercise is personal as these are the same tools I use to help myself mediate my own dreams. I hope you will find as much success using these tools as I have. I also hope that you will find it within yourself to believe in you… so much that you will fulfill every dream you will ever have.

Your Friend,
Lauren McGowen-Bond

A TIME TO BE PROUD OF:

President Obama Signed This. YAY!!!

Became a Triathlete

2015 Outstanding Athlete

2015 Inductee

Certified Peer Mental Coach

Ran 400m & 800m

It's kind of fun to
do the impossible
– Walt Disney

CHAPTER 1

Believing in Yourself

"People often ask me 'What do you want to be when you grow up?', and I think to myself, 'Why do I need to wait to grow up? Why can't I start being it today?'"

~ Lauren McGowen-Bond

ne question that has always bothered me is when people ask me, "What do you want to be when you grow up?" This bothers me because it makes it seem as if you have to be an older age to do great things. But you really don't need to be.

Really, no matter how old you are, you can start today!

Belief in Myself:

I wrote my first book at the age of 5. The reason I believed writing a book was possible was because it was in my blood. I have always been a bookworm who loved words and the world's they created in my mind. My mom is an author and watching her write, type and create her words seemed fun to me. So I thought to myself, "Why just sit here reading a book when I can write my own? Why not create a way for others to be inspired?" Even then, I believed I could inspire young people with my words. And I did not want to wait until I grew up in order to do it... I wanted to do it right then. So I did.

If I was unable to do what this book promises, to believe in myself, then you would not be reading it right now. I wrote this book because I want everyone reading it to know you can do whatever you put your mind to. I have a published book, and I'm only 10 years-old. That's proof that your age will never matter. But your mindset does.

I Had a Great Year:

In the beginning of this chapter I showed you some great things I have accomplished, both academically and athletically. But just imagine, if I believed what other people said about how you can only do great thing when your older, I would not have accomplished those things. If I did not believe I was capable of big things, they would never have occurred in my life. But since I did believe it, and never doubted myself because of my age, I was able to make my dreams come true.

Some of my greatest academic accomplishments are: An outstanding academic excellence certificate signed by president Barack Obama. Being inducted into National Elementary Honor Society. Making the honor roll every year since first grade. Being voted as student council representative for my class. Becoming a trained peer mediator for my school. And becoming a certified peer mental coach.

Some other cool things I have done are, I competed in the state Junior Olympics for the 400-meter dash and the 800-meter run. In the qualification round, I won first place in the 800 meter run and second place in the 400-meter dash. I am also an outstanding athlete in track and field for the Amateur Athletic Union (AAU). I also became a tri-athlete when I competed in my first kid's triathlon.

In the rest of this book, you will hear about more accomplishments I have made as proof that I believe in myself. Just know that I don't mean to brag in any way. All I am trying to do is let you know that you are capable of greatness and you can accomplish great things if you work hard for it. Because if I can do it, you can do it too!

Mediating Between Fear and Faith:

You need to have a positive attitude towards what you are trying to accomplish. As I talk about more in chapter 4, there are two parts to your brain: the left side and the right side. The left side is fear; it tries to protect you by convincing you that what you want to do is not possible. The right side is your beliefs. Your beliefs will push you forward and into those things you really want if you ignore the fear, take a risk, and give them a chance.

Lauren McGowen-Bond

You have to learn to mediate, or bring agreement, between these two sides of your brain in order for your dreams to come true. Over the years, I had to learn to mediate my dreams too. Sometimes it can be hard. However, you just need to have the right mindset in order to get through it. And that mindset is a bold and positive faith in yourself.

🐾 🐾 🐾

Don't Be a Victim:

Being a victim is when you make up excuses for not accomplishing greatness. And from things that I see, I know that being a victim is NOT a good thing. All it does is stop you from achieving excellence, and keeps you from living your dream. As a victim, the only thing you do is make people feel pitiful for you and that is SO not cool! So once again, don't be a victim!

🐾 🐾 🐾

Age Never Matters:

There are many examples of young people who accomplish big things at young ages. For instance, some of them win gold medals in the Olympics. Some sign with record labels and win Grammy's. There are young kids out there with IQ's higher than adult scientists who have PhD's. Youth who have created medical cures that doctors have not thought of yet. Kids who are just like you. The only thing that's different is these kids know they don't need to be older to be great because they can accomplish great things right now.

Remember this one important thing… if one person can do it, whatever it is, then you can do it too! No one is special. So, if the kids I mentioned earlier can do it… if I can do it…

4

then you can too! Mediate your belief in this area by making a commitment with yourself that you will begin to fulfill your goals and that you will never give up. Be confident and remember, you don't have to wait until you are older to start living your dreams; you can start living them today!

Lauren McGowen-Bond

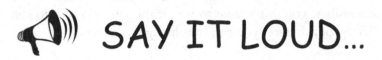

And an Elephant Would Never Forget It!!!

MEDIATION MOMENT:

CONTRACT WITH MYSELF – CHPT. 1

Believing in yourself means you are willing to do whatever you need to do in order to make your dreams come true. Both in good times and bad times.

For this exercise, you will need to sign a contract with yourself. This is your pledge to yourself. And remember, if you cannot keep your word to yourself, then what good is your word to others?

Grab your "I Believe in Me" journal, or get a piece of paper or a notebook, and go to Pages 75 for the exercise. Remember to sign and date the contract to make it valid.

WORDS TO LIVE BY – 1

Contract:
An agreement you make with yourself or another person. When you sign it, you are agreeing to honor your word and behave according to what is written.

Self-Belief:
Confidence in yourself and your abilities. Trusting in you and the things you can do.

Self-Esteem:
The way you feel about yourself because of your gifts and talents. The belief that you deserve the best for yourself and that you can do what it is you desire to do.

Victim Behavior:
Victims choose to believe they will always lose in life so they never have to try anything new or get their hopes up. Victims believe everything is against them, that life is unfair, and that others are better than they are. They use these feelings to get pity from others to feel powerful instead of stepping into being the powerful person they were meant to be. (Don't be a victim!).

CHAPTER 2

If You Believe It, You Can Achieve It!

1st Place Medals for Alpha Kappa Alpha Art & Writing Contest

"If you dream it, you can achieve it!"

~ Walt Disney

ne of my favorite things to tell myself when I am frustrated or am having trouble with something is, "If I believe it, I can achieve it." I actually say this to myself a lot. I said it when I was afraid while learning to swim so that I could participate in my first triathlon. I say it in school if I am

9

having a problem understanding the lesson. I say it when I am competing at track meets. Actually, I say it anytime I am learning something that is difficult or that seems hard for me to do.

Creating the Right Mindset:

In order to mediate your life so you can accomplish more, you have to create the right mindset. This means, you need to stop thinking negative or bad things about yourself or what you can do. When I struggle in this area, I give myself a pep-talk. I repeat a phrase over and over again until I am confident and ready to take on the challenge.

My mom teaches mindset and mental toughness to others. She helps people learn to create a belief in themselves that they can do whatever it is they put their minds to; even when bad things happen to them. One thing she always tells me is that the mind controls everything and it will always believe what I tell it. So, if I tell myself I cannot do something then I probably will not be able to do it. But if I tell myself that I can do something then the mind allows me to.

She also tells me that what our mind believes will create energy in our bodies; this energy will inspire action in us based on what we believe or have faith in. When we believe we can do something, our bodies have high energy and we are inspired to do the thing we most want to do. But if we believe that we cannot, then we have low energy and we will fear taking action and won't do anything productive. It is important for us to pay attention to the energy in our bodies because this will let us know when we need to change our beliefs.

Positive Self Talk:

I remember once I was taking the STAAR test in school. This is the state of Texas test for academic achievement. On this particular day, we were being tested in reading comprehension. This is actually my favorite subject, but I really did not want to take the test that day. I was afraid I was going to do badly. Every time I thought this, my eyes would get really tired and my body felt sleepy. While I was reading, I was so out of it that I was not understanding or comprehending what I was reading. I also noticed I was getting the answers slowly; way slower than I normally do.

During the test, I decided to give myself a positive self-talk. This is when you talk to yourself and say really positive things. The cool thing is that because it's positive, it creates high energy. During my talk I began to chant, "I can do this. I can do this. I can do this." I also told myself repeatedly "If I believe it then I can achieve it and get a good grade." I immediately began to feel different. I noticed that my eyes opened up more, my body sat up straighter and I had more energy and paid attention. I was excited to get the test finished.

When the test results came back, my mom was so proud of me. I was proud of myself too. I received commended performance on the test because I only missed two questions on the entire reading section. And even though I knew it before, I learned my mom was right. The mind really does control everything. Would I have passed the test if I had not done the chanting? I'm sure I would have. But I know I would not have done as well because it changed everything about my energy and what I believed I could do. The chanting helped me to feel empowered and reminded me to always believe in me!

Lauren McGowen-Bond

<u>Negative Chatter from Others</u>:

One of the most important things to remember is there will always be people who will try to convince you that you cannot do or have something. They are low energy people. They will listen to you talk about a dream you have or what you want to accomplish and will say to you, "Oh, that can't happen to you in reality." But it can happen. If you believe in your dreams they will come true. But if you create low energy in your body, you won't perform as well as you could have and they will not.

<u>Chanting as Mediation for Beliefs:</u>

Dreams are all about believing in them. However, the mind controls everything and belief is formed first in the mind. You would not be reading this book right now if not for your mind. It will <u>always</u> believe what you say. Therefore, it will also believe any negative things others may say about you if it already agrees with or believes the exact thing they are saying. This is why you have to protect your belief in yourself... even if the person you are protecting yourself from is you.

Remember, if you say you cannot do something, or if you believe others when they say you cannot do something, then the mind will believe it and it most likely will not happen. You have to remember to pay attention to your energy. You also have to control what you say and hear about your dreams as this is important to how you believe in yourself.

I believe in me because I know I have the power to make things happen. When you believe in you, you will have the power to make things happen for you too. Belief gives you the ability to mediate your fears and change your life. Chanting, "I can do it", makes me feel like a whole new person. I feel happy and empowered when I believe in me. You can mediate for yourself to feel happy and empowered too. It's simple; all you have to do is chant the words, "I believe in me!"

At Awards Ceremony

School Spelling Bee

My Friend Ty & I at Triathlon
Swim·Bike·Run

13

Lauren McGowen-Bond

And an Elephant Would Never Forget It!!!

MEDIATION MOMENT:

YES, I CAN!!! – CHPT. 2

Positive self-talk is important for making your dreams come true. This exercise will help you change your mindset from what you believe you cannot do to what you believe you can.

Grab your "I Believe in Me" journal, or get a piece of paper, or notebook and go to Pages 76-77 for the exercise.

WORDS TO LIVE BY – 2

Mindset:
The habits and parts of your beliefs that determine how you will respond to different situations in life.

Purpose:
A goal to be achieved. Your life is one big goal – that special something you are sent to earth to achieve.

Positive Self-Talk:
A conversation that takes place in your head where you cheer yourself on to change the way you think and behave.

Chant:
Words you say in rhythm, over and over again, to inspire yourself to believe a certain way about something.

CHAPTER 3

Don't Give Your Power Away

"You are braver than you believe and stronger than you
seem and smarter than you think."

~ Winnie the Pooh

One of the most important lessons to learn is not
to give others the power over you to make you
feel less than who you are. Even if this person is
a friend or a family member, you should not allow
them or their actions against you to bring you
down. This is important because it's hard to believe in yourself
when you allow someone else to control how you feel. If
someone else controls how you feel, then it's hard to feel
empowered. And if you don't feel empowered, it's difficult to

17

go after your dreams.

♂ ♂ ♂

They Tried to Take My Power:

There was a girl in my class who I thought was my friend. She used to make fun of me in so many ways: What I wore. How I wore my hair. How I did not have the new Air Jordan's or something she thought was popular. And she was always mean to me when she did it. I felt bad at first because she was supposed to be my friend. But then I saw that whenever I felt bad she felt better. She felt empowered while I felt like crying. And I did not like that feeling, so I realized I needed to learn to keep my power.

There is another girl who really is my friend. But, if I don't want to do what she wants me to do, she stops talking to me She ignores me until she either gets her way, or we find something to do that she likes. Sometimes, I feel like she only wants to be my friend because I'm younger than she is and she thinks she can get me to do what she wants me to do. But other times, when we both want to do the same thing, we have a lot of fun together and it's great.

♂ ♂ ♂

Maintaining Your Personal Power:

I realize now that when people talk down to me, or when they talk negatively to me, or when they pout or get upset, they want to control me or the situation. And if I let them, this is another form of me giving my power away. So, I had to learn not to allow other people's needs or feelings to get me down. I also had to learn to never compromise to the point where I don't have fun or get to do the things I want to do.

I learned to encourage myself instead of waiting for friends or anyone else to encourage me. Doing this helped me to no longer care about what they thought or what they wanted. I realized they were using manipulation and pouting to influence me to do what they wanted me to do. I was then able to move forward and find the healthy me again.

Do not let other people bring you down. Also, do not allow others to manipulate you. I no longer allow anyone, even my friends, to manipulate me into doing what they want me to do. I learned to believe in me and I now realize that I matter just as much as they do. You do not have to do what others tell you to do. Do what you feel is right for you and never let others control you. You have a perfectly good mind of your own... so make sure you use it!

🐕 🐕 🐕

Maintain Control at All Times:

When someone is trying to take your power, the best thing to do is ignore them and let it go. You should focus on you and not them. Do not let them, or what they are saying or doing, get to you. Just forget about it because again, the reason that person is making fun of you is they want to have your power. If you stay in control, you will be the one with the power, not them.

In the past, whenever someone tried to take my power, I used to argue back with them and fight with them. But I realized that yelling at the person was unnecessary and it did not get us anywhere. So I started doing an exercise that I learned from my art teacher. The purpose of this exercise is to help you heal the hurt you felt from someone else's actions so you can begin to feel good again.

Lauren McGowen-Bond

Mediating My Moments:

The first thing I do is write some of my feelings on a sheet of paper. When I am done, I tear the paper up and throw away the pieces. It is now as if the bad stuff that was said about me is gone. Then, on a clean piece of paper, I write down good things about myself. Some of the things I write are, "I AM smart", "I AM beautiful", and I AM amazing". This exercise helps to heal my hurt and makes me feel better by seeing the positive things about me. Writing down good things is what helps me mediate my feelings. After doing this exercise, I see that I am no longer mad, sad, hurt or depressed.

This exercise is great because it focuses on you instead of the other person. There are other things you may want to do in this situation, like fight back with words or actions, but those things could make you feel just as powerless as you felt in the first place. Let's say you want to yell at the other person. It might temporarily make you feel better, but they would still have taken your power because they were able to control you. They were able to get you from being calm to being angry.

Or, you might always want to run and tell an adult. And yes, telling an adult is a great thing to do and is really what you should do. But, this might make you feel powerless too. You could begin to feel like a tattletale and like you need someone else to fight your battles. That's why this exercise is a great mediation tool.

Mediating the life of your dreams includes refusing to allow others to bring you down. You cannot allow them to make you feel bad about yourself. And you should never give them your power. You were born to be powerful. And you are powerful... just the way you are. I believe this and this is why I believe in me. When you learn to remember this at all times you will always believe in you too!

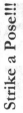

Strike a Pose!!!

And an Elephant Would Never Forget It!!!

MEDIATION MOMENT:

REDEEMING YOUR POWER – CHPT. 3

Feeling powerless, or **_dis_**-empowered, means you have pulled away from your own inner ability to create the life you really want.

This exercise will help you to feel better and to reconnect to your power. It will also help to restore the powerful things you believe about yourself deep down.

Grab your "I Believe in Me" journal or get a piece of paper or notebook and go to Pages 78-79 for the exercise.

WORDS TO LIVE BY - 3

<u>**Personal Power**</u>:

Being able to influence yourself and your actions even when things do not seem to be going your way.

<u>**Self-Empowerment**</u>:

To give power and authority to yourself to believe in your dreams. To believe you are powerful enough as you are – right now – to live the amazing life you want to live.

<u>**Mental Toughness**</u>:

The ability to bounce back from mistakes and disappointments even stronger than you were before.

CHAPTER 4

Don't Wait! Your Dreams Begin Now!

"If you don't see the book you want on the shelf, write it!"
~ Beverly Clearly

hen people ask me, "What do you want to be when you grow up?" it always makes me think, "Grow up... grow up?! Why do you have to wait until you grow up? Why can't you find out what you want and start being and doing it today?"

25

Lauren McGowen-Bond

Be Proud of Your Achievements:

I wrote my first children's book when I was still in kindergarten. It's called "The Princess and the Panda." I was inspired while watching my mom write her book and I actually completed it in one weekend. It is still unpublished as we are looking for an illustrator, but I'm extremely proud that I wrote it. I'm proud that I saw something I wanted to do and did it.

I am now ten years old. I am a national elementary scholar, a state recognized athlete, a triathlete, a certified peer mental coach and a trained peer mediator for my school. I have received countless high achieving academic awards, competed at state track competitions, won 1st place in art and writing competitions, and received medals for science fairs. And just recently, I was invited to be a part of the 'Outstanding Athletes of AAU 2015 Edition." That's pretty cool!

I have achieved a host of other things too and the amazing thing is I am just getting started. I do not want to make it seem as if I am bragging. I just want you to know that if I can do this, or anything like it, then you can too. I am proud of my achievements. Had I waited until I grew up to do big things, I feel like I would be behind because I do not believe I was ever supposed to wait. And neither are you!

Find Activities that Tie Into Your Dreams:

Being a trained peer mediator is incredible! My school is amazing in that they allowed elementary-aged students to participate in this program. This made me feel pretty special to know that I am one of the chosen ones. Our school district invested in our opportunity and we were trained to do the same work that older kids and adults are doing. In this position, we are like mini-counselors, or social workers, helping peers find a resolution to problems in their school day.

This is also great because it mimics what I want to do in my life and what this book is about. I want to help young people find a way to mediate their dreams. I want to be their mental coach. I want to help them find solutions to their problems in life so these problems don't have a way of stopping them from living their dreams. And I already started.

Creating Your Own Opportunities:

You would think that I would need to be older to have the titles of both Peer Mental Coach and Peer Mediator. But programs like this exist everywhere. It's just that many kids either do not know opportunities like this exist or simply do not believe they exist for them. Their mind limits them because it bases the ability to achieve on age. When really, age is nothing but a number. It should never factor into whether or not you believe in creating your dreams.

No matter what someone may tell you, you are never too young to achieve big things. People who think that kids cannot realize big accomplishments are wrong. I said this before: there are youth in the world who are competing in professional competitions, both academic and athletic. They are making discoveries in all areas, and are doing other big things. They are not waiting for the "right age". They are simply creating moments to accomplish their dreams right now. And you can too! Whatever is possible for one person is possible for all – as long as the person has the mindset to believe it then regardless of their age they can absolutely achieve it.

Lauren McGowen-Bond

Don't Let Others Change Your Direction:

When you are mediating your dreams, you also have to remember not to allow others to change them. When I wrote my first book, my mother tried to change a lot of my thoughts and ideas in the book. I don't think it was because she thought what I wrote was bad. I think she was being a mom and wanted to help me make it better. Plus, she's a writer and an editor so editing was second nature for her. But I liked what I wrote. So, as politely as possible I told her, "That's a good idea, but I want to keep it the way that it is." I was comfortable enough in my dreams and my Purpose that I would not allow even my mom to change what the book was supposed to be. And thankfully she understood.

My mom always says I came into this world knowing what I was supposed to be and that it is simply her job to make sure what I want comes to pass. She only wants to help prepare me to fulfill the purpose I came into this world to fulfill and nothing different. She does not push me to be something I am not meant to be. Instead she tells me that even though I am young I have to be willing to fight for what I know to be true and right in my life. What I learned from her is that, even at my young age, I cannot allow others to limit me and tell me I cannot do or accomplish something. And most importantly, I cannot allow others to change who or what I become. That I have to always believe in me! I am glad that she understands and teaches me this because it is a great requirement for mediating your dreams.

You Really Can Start Right Now:

I wrote this chapter because I really want you to know that though you might be young, there are major things you can do to live some part of your dreams right now today! I have seen kids as young as four and five years old compete in competitions, get gold medals, and win. It's like when I saw my mom writing her book, I saw that as something I was supposed to do so I did it. I did not wait until I got older. In doing that, I learned that my age did not matter. What mattered was that I had a good mindset and that I believed that I could.

Today, I'm no longer surprised or shocked when I accomplish anything. I am mostly just happy when I do. The reason is because I learned to expect great things to happen to me. You should too! And when you begin to regularly mediate the life of your dreams, you will. I know that age is nothing but a number; and this is why I can believe in me! Forget about your age, stop waiting until you're older, and believe in you too! And remember, if you don't see what you want to be in the world then create it. The world just might be waiting on you to turn that dream into reality.

Lauren McGowen-Bond

MEDIATION MOMENT:

EXPECTING GREATNESS – CHPT. 4

The 'Expecting Greatness' exercise is adapted from an exercise that my mom taught my classmates and I in 1st grade.

The exercise is called "Choices for Change". This exercise inspires you to **expect greatness** in your life. When you do, you will shape your behavior so you can have the life you want.

Grab your "I Believe in Me" journal, or get a piece of paper or notebook, and go to Pages 80-81 for the exercise.

WORDS TO LIVE BY – 4

Feeling Accomplished:
When you feel you have done your best in a task or mission that you completed.

Achievements:
Goals that have been successfully completed with great effort and in the face of difficulty.

Age:
The number of years a person has been alive. This is not a determining factor of if you should live your dreams.

Expectation:
A strong belief that something will happen. The mental attitude to know that you can achieve success.

Destiny:
A course of events that will happen in the future. Your life is destined to happen a certain way. You simply just need to do the work to make it happen and believe it.

CHAPTER 5

Be Afraid. Just Don't Give UP!

"Don't give up, I believe in you all. A person's a person no matter how small."

~ Dr. Seuss

Yes, the title of this chapter is correct. It really is okay to be afraid. Being young and looking to accomplish big things can seem scary. But, it's really not a bad thing to feel the fear that comes up in your life. What would be bad though was if you allowed that fear to force you to give up. It would be bad if you allowed it to stop you from living your dreams.

Lauren McGowen-Bond

Fear – The Big Bully:

Fear can be a scary thing. It's like a bully living inside of your brain. It usually begins by teasing you when you are about to do or accomplish something new. Its job is to make you feel like you will not be able to accomplish your goals. It tells you things like, "You can't do that," or "You're a chicken." When really, it's wrong. You can do or accomplish what you are trying to do. Just don't feel bad; you're not the only person who fear is able to make feel this way. The key though is to learn to mediate your fears so you can stop fear from succeeding in the future. Because trust me, it will try every day!

     🐕 🐕 🐕

Achieving Even When You're Afraid:

I remember one of the times I almost let fear win. It was when I needed to learn to swim so I could participate in my first triathlon. I was afraid of the water because it seemed spooky to me. I was afraid to trust it, but knew I had to or my dreams of being a triathlete would die. So, I did not have a choice – I was afraid but had to learn to swim anyway.

When I started my lessons, I used to scream if the coach tried to make me float by myself or if he let me go. I was so afraid that I used to cry. My mother once told me that water was dangerous and that being afraid meant not thinking which meant I could die. This made me feel worse. However, I had a dream. So, I went to swim lessons 3x a week and gave it my all.

I only had around 6 weeks before the triathlon to learn to swim, which was not a lot of time given how terrified I was of the water. But I never gave up. In April of 2015, I participated in my first Kid's Triathlon sponsored by the Houston Texans.

And because I kept moving forward and allowed the fear to push me instead of stop me I can now call myself a tri-athlete.

Two Sides of Our Brain:

I like to call fear a "Big blob of nothing." This means that although the fear might seem really big and heavy, it's only purpose is to make you believe you can't do something that you probably can do. It controls you by making you feel unprepared. It tells you that other people are better than you or that people will make fun of you. It also makes you believe you will be hurt if you try something new, or worse, that you will die. And when you listen, it wins.

I like to say there are two parts to our brains; a positive side and a negative side. The positive side is where you are confident and sure you can be successful. This side stores all the things you want to achieve and accomplish. The negative side is where your fear lives. This side stores all the things you think you can't do as well as all the voices of the people who say you cannot accomplish big things.

The negative side of our brains is like our own personal bully. It wants to control you but you cannot let it. You cannot allow it to get to you because you won't move forward or accomplish your goals. And this would mean that the bully won. The best thing to do is to treat it like you would any other bully. You should ignore it and remind yourself that you are a great person capable of great things. But whatever you do, do not let it win.

Lauren McGowen-Bond

Learning From Our Fears:

Having fear is not all bad, but it does hold you back from doing what you want to do. You can learn from it though. Think of those times when you know you wanted to do something but instead you made up excuses as to why you could not do it. Then, when the event was over you regretted not participating. You were upset with yourself because you should not have allowed fear to win. Moments like these teach you that if you want something you should keep pushing yourself. I know for a fact how bad it feels to let fear win. But I also know you can always do something if you ignore your fears and put your mind to it.

🐎 🐎 🐎

How to Mediate Fear and Faith:

At some point in your life you will find yourself stuck inside the blob of fear. The best way to mediate this is to continue to go after the dreams and goals you set for yourself - even when you are afraid. If you believe in yourself, it does not matter how much fear you have. The positive side is much stronger than the negative side. Good energy makes you feel that you can accomplish anything. Good energy will make you believe you can and you will accomplish big things.

The way I mediate these two sides is by doing my confidence exercises. I repeat to myself, over and over again, that "I can do it". I really do believe that I can do whatever it is I put my mind to. However, chanting it makes me feel more confident. It helps to ease my fears or calm them down so I can accomplish my goals.

Today, I'm still not entirely 100% comfortable in the water. But I'm getting better every day. I learned to swim and became a tri-athlete because although I was afraid, I did not let the fear win. I unleashed my inner champion. I am extremely proud of myself for that. Just remember to unleash your inner champion whenever you are afraid and you will always be proud of yourself too!

Lauren McGowen-Bond

And an Elephant Would Never Forget It!!!

MEDIATION MOMENT:

I DARE YOU! – CHPT. 5

Daring yourself to try something new is the perfect way to mediate your fears. It allows you to practice feeling the fear but doing it anyway.

This mediation moment will dare you to challenge yourself. Have fun! And remember to break out of your comfort zone!

Grab your "I Believe in Me" journal, or get a piece of paper, or notebook, and go to Pages 82-83 for the exercise.

WORDS TO LIVE BY - 5

Fear:

Fear is false information that presents itself as truth in order for the mind to protect us from being hurt. Fear is NOT REAL! It just feels that way!

Acronym for FEAR to Motivate You:

(F) False
(E) Evidence
(A) Appearing
(R) Real

*This means fear shows you something or makes you feel or believe something to get you to believe it's true. But it isn't. Like any good magic trick, it's just an illusion.

Faith:

A strong belief or trust. Believing something is true with everything in you. Having faith in yourself means you believe you can accomplish anything you set your mind to. Also, that you trust in your abilities with everything you have.

CHAPTER 6

No Excuses... PERIOD!

"When life gives you an excuse, give it back... you don't need it!"

~ Tonoa Bond (my mom)

O ne of the most important reasons you have for believing in yourself is this: When you believe your dreams are possible you will not allow yourself to make excuses. Even if something bad happens to you, you will not allow that one bad thing to convince you it is okay to give up. Instead, you will push forward and make your dreams happen because you totally believe they can come true no matter what!

Excuse or Little White Lie:

I see excuses as nothing but lies you tell yourself, or another person, to get out of doing something. Think of a time when you made an excuse and failed to do something you really wanted to do. A time when you were being lazy or when you were scared that you would not be successful. How did you feel after that opportunity was gone? Like you could have or should have at least tried to achieve it, right? Giving yourself a reason to live beneath your potential will never help you to believe in yourself and your dreams.

When I make an excuse, I feel bad. I feel like I'm wasting my time and my opportunities. And if it's something that my mom had to spend money on for me to participate in, or something that someone else had to make happen for me, I feel like I am letting them down too. And that does not feel good to me.

The No-Excuse Mindset:

When you go after your dreams, you have to have a determined and hard-working mindset. You have to have a mindset where you will not let yourself give up. If you don't, then you will make excuses all the time. Remember, an excuse is nothing but a lie that you allow in your life so you won't have to live up to your potential. When you make-up lies about your possibilities, or if you don't have the mindset to believe in yourself, then what you're really doing is telling yourself that you don't want big things. Or even scarier, that you don't deserve them. And you won't get anywhere in life if you let excuses guide your way.

I recently read a story in school about a woman named April Holmes. Ms. Holmes is a USA Paralympic track and field athlete who had her left leg amputated after a horrible train accident. She spent nine months recovering in the hospital and learning to walk again. During that time, she was making plans to run again as well. You see, Ms. Holmes has been an athlete since she was 5 years old. She was a high school and college track star and running was all she knew. So, after her accident, she refused to accept the lie, or make the excuse, that because she lost her leg she would never be able to run again.

After Ms. Holmes was fitted with a prosthetic leg, she began to make her goals a reality. She raced in the Paralympics games (a major sporting event featuring athletes with disabilities) and began to set records in the 100m sprint. She could have made excuses as to why her dreams of running or competing again were over. She could have told herself that having a prosthetic leg meant she would never be fast again. But she refused to give in to her disability and she persevered. Today, she now helps others to believe in themselves so they can persevere too. Ms. Holmes once said, "When you fall down, you have to get up and keep going." She is absolutely right! Bad things happen in life. But it is amazing when a person falls and gets right back up.

Never Give Up:

There are so many others who are like Ms. Holmes. They have also had bad things happen to them but never gave up on their dreams or stopped believing in themselves. There are kids who get really sick, but still fight. There are people who have no role models, but they refuse to let that stop them. These people inspire me because they push through their hardships and tragedies every day. They don't take no for an answer and don't take anything for granted.

I have a friend and classmate named Jramail who got really sick. He had cancer and was in the hospital for almost a year. During that time, he still studied and excelled in school. While in the hospital receiving chemotherapy – and fighting for his life – he took the state achievement test and got commended performance in every subject. We were also inducted into the National Elementary Honor Society together. He inspires me as he is a true example of the 'no excuses' mindset.

My mom is another example of the 'no excuses' mindset. She never allows me to make excuses for anything. She doesn't accept them and I understand. Excuses are a waste of my time and hers. She's taught me that excuses don't do anything to push my life forward. So, why would I lie to myself and make excuses when I can be doing something great instead?!

You have to fight for the things you want in life. Mediating your dreams means you cannot allow anyone, not even yourself, to give you an excuse that stops you from fulfilling your goals. You have to work for your dreams regardless of what's happening. You have to develop the mindset to not let fear tell you that what you want isn't possible. Your positive side needs to push you forward. This is the only way you'll be able to mediate for your dreams.

Impossible Means I AM Possible:

Nothing is ever impossible. When you believe things are

impossible, you tend to give up. 'Impossible' seems like such a powerful word. But if you look at it closely, you will see that it can actually be split into two words, Im-Possible or "I'm possible". Whenever you have challenges in life, never say that what you want is "Im-Possible." Instead, look at the challenges, add an apostrophe, and say "I'm possible" or "I AM POSSIBLE". Because you are!

When excuses come, I mediate them with a mindset exercise. The words "I AM" are two of the most powerful words in the universe. They help you create a powerful mindset because whatever comes after these words the mind automatically believes. Creating "I AM" statements is a great mediation exercise. These affirmations help you believe what you want is possible. And when you believe this, you refuse to accept excuses. Now is the time for you to believe in you, always and forevermore, because you ARE possible!

Lauren McGowen-Bond

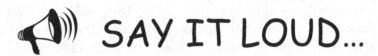

And an Elephant Would Never Forget It!!!

MEDIATION MOMENT:

I AM... POSSIBLE! – CHPT. 6

"I AM" are two of the most powerful words in the Universe because what follows these words the mind automatically believes. This exercise will help you realize that nothing is impossible as long as you believe in yourself and your dreams.

Grab your "I Believe in Me" journal, or get a piece of paper, or notebook, and go to Pages 84-85 for the exercise.

WORDS TO LIVE BY – 6

Excuses:

Lies you tell yourself or others that give you permission to live beneath your potential. Remember, excuses stop you from living your dreams. So, don't make them, okay?!

Perseverance:
Continuing to achieve something you want in the face of fear. When you persevere, you are saying to yourself and the world you refuse to give up on your dreams!

Determination:
To come to the decision that you are going to fight through any problems you might have so you can accomplish your dreams. It is the bravery and mental strength you need to live up to your potential.

Ability:
The physical, mental and intellectual power you need to perform at your best. The personal skills, talents and gifts you have to change the world.

CHAPTER 7

We All Have Haters! Dream Big Anyway!

"Don't tell me the sky is the limit when I see footprints on the moon."

~ The Dalai Lama

There will always be someone in your life that hates on you or what you do. These people will want to stop you from being your best or having something great in your life. But why should they matter? Why should they be allowed to steal your celebrations from you? YOU are the pirate of your own ship.

So you should never allow anyone to tell you what you are or are not good at!

Hater vs Support System:

A hater is someone who doesn't believe in themselves so they want you not to believe in yourself either. They actually feel empowered when they hate, criticize, or belittle others. They need you to feel as bad about yourself as they feel about themselves so they won't struggle alone. If they can get you to stop believing in yourself, they win. But do you want THEM to win? I know I don't. This is why you need to support yourself. And the best way to do this is to ask for help.

When you have big dreams for your life, you need a support system. It's kind of like having a family just for your dreams. It's filled with people who are able to help you and give you very good advice and tips on how to get good at what you want to do. I have a lot of people in my life who do this for me. My strongest support comes from my mom as she always pushes me to do my best and reminds me that I can do anything I set my mind to. I also have support in my prior teachers. Having the support of others is important because when the haters come in your life, or when other people try to stop you from succeeding, your support system can fight for you when you cannot fight for yourself.

Finding Others to Support You:

When I first moved to Texas from California, I was a grade ahead of what the school system in Texas believed I should have been. This is because California had a different age requirement to start school. So, I started first grade when I was still only five years old. The school district in Texas felt that because of my age I should have been in kindergarten. They gave my mom a hard time and tried to put me back into kindergarten. They told her I was too young and because of their laws there was nothing she could do to stop them. But my mom never takes no for an answer. So she made a lot of phone calls – a lot of phone calls - and was able to fight the system. And when school started, I was in the first grade.

My mom supported my growth and learning and did not allow me to repeat kindergarten. This was a good thing too because I was already reading on a 4th grade level and could spell the same words my cousins were spelling in 6th grade. So going back to kindergarten would have been really boring for me. But had she not fought that battle, and accepted what they said instead, back in kindergarten is where I would have been.

Later that year, my first grade teacher realized I was advanced and would send me to the advanced class for reading and writing. She then recommended me for the advanced track for second grade. This wouldn't have happened if I been put in kindergarten instead of her class. This teacher still supports my other gifts and talents by constantly encouraging me. She believes in me and always inspires me to believe in me too.

The next year, my second grade teacher had to fight for my place in the school talent show. She felt that my audition was better than some of the students who actually made it. They made me the emcee of the show, but she still was not happy. She pushed until they gave me the spot I earned. And guess what? I was able to do both; I got to emcee as well as be a contestant. I got to do so much more than I'd originally auditioned for simply because I had someone who believed in and supported me. Without her, I would have been sitting on the sidelines watching others do something I, myself, had dreamed of doing.

Being Your Own Biggest Supporter:

If you don't have people in your life who believe in you then it's really important for you to learn to believe in yourself. You have to learn to be your own support system when you are accomplishing big things. Every year, from first through fourth grade, I asked my mom if I could participate in the triathlon and every year she told me no. Mainly because I did not know how to ride a bike and because I could not swim. But in fourth grade she realized she was wrong for stopping my dream. So, because I continued to believe in my dream she got me the training I needed to compete.

Had it not been for my belief in myself, I would not have competed in the triathlon. Every year, when I saw the triathlon flyer, I saw myself running past the finish line and getting a medal. So I pushed myself and never allowed anything, even my mom saying 'no,' to stop me. I completed my first triathlon basically because I believed in me and never gave up.

Finding Support by Mirroring Others:

What if you don't have any encouragement in your environment or anyone who can offer you support? What if you are feeling so down you are unable to support yourself? This is when you find someone to mirror. This means, you find someone who is better than you are at something and you use them and their actions as a guide to how you should behave.

I have a friend who always excels. She's gifted in academics, arts, and music and is always chosen to represent our school in some way. She is one of the people I set my benchmark to. The bar she set for herself is high and I want to meet her at it and exceed it. This is healthy competition because I don't want to beat her just to say I beat her or to hurt her. I want to do better than her because she is doing more than average or mediocre things. She always excels at a high level and I want to push myself to excel at a high level too.

I remember one day while I was doing my homework my mom got irritated with me. I wasn't concentrating very well and was upset that my homework was taking me so long. She told me she was noticing a change in both my study habits and my attitude towards school and she did not like it. During our talk, she repeated this phrase to me a few times… "You are around average people every day, and somehow their actions or beliefs are convincing you that it's okay for you to be average too. Are you okay with this?" Sitting there and hearing that, I realized that I wasn't.

My mom wasn't telling me that my peers were bad people or that I was better than them. She was just telling me that I was starting to fit in with the crowd instead of being a leader. Mirroring the actions of someone who is excelling helps to move me out of settling for whatever comes my way and forces me to fight for what I want. I never want to be average; I want to be exceptional. And I will as long as I continue to believe it.

Mediation as a Support:

Sometimes your dreams will be so big you won't be able to do them by yourself. You might decide to give up on your dreams before you make it to the finish line. Or maybe someone will say you're not good enough and give your spot to others. You need a support team to help you live up to your potential. This means you need to believe in yourself so much that you self-advocate. This means you are able to ask for help or find the help that's required. Because, when you find a team of people who believe in you, it becomes very easy to believe in you too!

Mom & I After President's Awards

My Cousin Teaching Me to Skate

My Big Brother: Big Wolf & Lil Wolf

SAY IT LOUD...

I AM
AMAZING!

And an Elephant Would Never Forget It!!!

MEDIATION MOMENT:

ADVOCATING FOR YOUR DREAMS – CHPT. 7

This mediation will include a list of three options as there are many ways to advocate for yourself. The key is to find the most authentic one that fits with your situation.

Grab your "I Believe in Me" journal, or get a piece of paper, or notebook, and go to Pages 86-87 for the exercise.

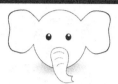

WORDS TO LIVE BY – 7

Hater/Enemy:

A person who feels empowered when they hate on, criticize, or belittle others. Someone who wants you to believe you cannot accomplish big dreams or goals.

Support (Or Support System):

People who offer you love, encouragement and support to let you know they believe in you and your dreams.

Self-Advocate:

Believing in yourself so much you are able ask for help. Standing up for yourself and what you believe no matter who is against you.

Average/Mediocre Mindset:

Not living up to your potential. Refusing to live an exceptional life. Choosing to fit in. Not believing you can have more out of life.

CHAPTER 8

Find What You're Good At and Do It!

"Everybody has a purpose in life and my purpose is to help people."

~ April Holmes

I wrote this book because I wanted to share ways for you to believe in yourself and mediate your dreams. Also, because I like to write, I believe I am good at it, and I did not want to wait until I was a grown up before I shared this message with you. I learned early what my purpose was and I decided to do it! My age did not matter. And this is the goal of this book. To help you discover whatever it is you are good at and take the steps you need to start living that dream now.

$$\textit{ਸ਼ ਸ਼ ਸ਼}$$

<u>Steps to Living Your Dreams:</u>

I believe there are four steps we should take to live our dreams. A couple of these steps have been mentioned in the previous chapters of this book. However, the others are easy to understand without needing explanation. These steps are:

Step 1: Find What You Are Good at and Do It. Knowing what you want to do is important because that's where you begin. If you don't know what you want to be, to have or to do, then you will never accomplish anything. Once you know what your "it" is, you will then give yourself permission to move to the next step.

Step 2: Find a Support System. As I said earlier in the book, a big dream will always need support. Yes, you are the pirate of your own ship, but even those in charge need people to help them steer the ship and keep it on track. So, remember to advocate for yourself and find your support team; even if that person is you. Once you have it, you can move on to the next step.

Step 3: Study or Find a Coach to Train You. It is extremely important that you give yourself a chance to become good at what you want to do. This means, studying whatever subjects you need to study, finding someone to mentor you, and accepting criticism from others. Sometimes it's hard to accept training from others because it also comes with some form of criticism. But, you have to do it knowing that the training, as well as their words, are only going to make you better.

Step 4: Make it happen. This is absolutely the most important part in making your dreams come to life! You have to do something that completes a goal or step to achieve that dream. If you are a couch potato, you won't get anything done. You have to be active and determined and try your best in order to make your dreams happen!

Maintaining Your Identity:

One of the most important parts of finding what you are good at is first knowing who you are. When you believe in yourself it means you have taken the time to identify who you are and what you want. You can only believe you are possible when you know what you represent to the world. This means, being willing to see your total picture: Who you are, what you are good at, and how your actions are either hurting or helping you (are they pushing you forward or pulling you back?). And most importantly, you have to be honest about how you show yourself to the world.

Learning What You Are Not Good At:

Finding what you are good at also means knowing what you are <u>not</u> good at. You have to know those things you are still learning so you can give yourself permission to perfect them. This is how you will build confidence in your talents.

My cousin Jason is an amazing person. He has autism, but is never afraid to try new things. However, he will also let you know when he doesn't trust your abilities. One day we were swimming at the neighborhood pool. I asked him if he wanted me to hold him in the water, but he frowned and said "No, you swim." And even though I'd just learned to swim and was still afraid to go out of 4 feet, I tried to prove to him I knew what I was doing. Instead, I sank and ended up with a mouth full of water. Afterward, sounding confident, I asked him, "How was that? Will you go in the water with me now?" He frowned his face, turned his head, and said, "No!", then walked away.

I actually don't blame him. If that were me, and someone messed up while they were doing something I was afraid of, I would not trust them either. When I thought about it later, I realized I was so busy trying to prove to Jason I was a good swimmer that I forgot to focus on those things I needed to learn to perfect. I am not a good swimmer. I am a beginning swimmer. I'm still learning. And that's okay. I know that I don't have to be good at swimming, I just need to be good at learning and the rest will come.

🐫 🐫 🐫

Recap:

I think it's clear that this book is about believing in yourself. Why? Because I think this is the best way to mediate your dreams. When you have self-belief it means you give yourself permission to find what you are good at and do it to the best of your abilities. Like I've said a million times, the mind follows what you tell it to do. So when you believe in yourself, you make what you believe come true.

Just remember your four steps to success:
1. Discover what you are good at or what you want to do.
2. Find a support system
3. Get the training you need – study or find a coach
4. Make it happen!

And lastly, don't be afraid to dream too big. There is nothing, and I mean absolutely nothing, that is impossible! Why? Because you are bigger than impossible... YOU ARE POSSIBLE! You just have to be willing to mediate your fear and faith at all times. And if you forget how, or if things get too hard, it's going to be okay. Just sit still, close your eyes, and confidently chant the password out loud... "I Believe in Me!"

My Cousin Jason & I

Lauren McGowen-Bond

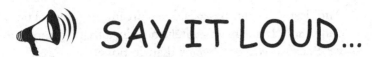 SAY IT LOUD...

I BELIEVE
IN ME!

And an Elephant Would Never Forget It!!!

MEDIATION MOMENT:

DREAMING WITH YOUR EYES OPEN – CHPT. 8

This chapter's Mediation Moment is super-sized – just as your dreams should be. There are two exercises to help you to believe in your dreams regardless of whatever is coming against you.

Dreaming with your eyes open requires that you form your identity. That you believe in yourself and believe that your dreams can come true. And that you do this even when the world seems to be against you. Let's create a dream (identity) board and a calming jar!

So… Grab your "I Believe in Me" journal, or get a piece of paper, or notebook, and go to Pages 88-89 for the exercise.

WORDS TO LIVE BY – 8

<u>**Identity:**</u>
The part of you that makes up who you are, how you think about yourself, the way the world sees you and the things about you that define you.

<u>**Closure:**</u>
Bring something to an end or conclusion. Accepting that you have to remove yourself from situations that do not help you to grow.

<u>**Living a Resigned Life:**</u>
Living everyday as if you know your dreams are expected or inescapable. Accepting your greatness. Showing behavior every day that places you closer to the things you want to accomplish.

<u>**Nurturing Yourself and Your Dreams:**</u>
Feeding, training and developing in yourself the skills, talents and intellect you need to live the most amazing life ever!

THE BELIEVER'S CREED
Adapted from "The Learner's Creed"
By: Ernestine Stewart Mitchell

We say 'The Learner's Creed' every day at school. It is one of my favorite exercises as it inspires me to be better. Although the original words are perfect, I added a few of my own to inspire you to believe in yourself and to be better too!

I believe in myself and in my ability

To do my best at all times

I am intelligent

I am capable of greatness

Just for today

I will listen

I will see

I will speak

I will feel

I will think

I will reason

I will read

I will write

I WILL BELIEVE!

I will do all these things

With one purpose in mind

To do and believe in my very best

And to not waste this day

For this day will come no more.

AFTERWORD

I remember the first time I saw her. Her eyes were so bright. Not because they caught the light, but because an explosive desire glowed from within.

Lauren was mature in a sense that she got the bigger picture in life, but still precious enough to be impressionable by the wonders around her. She could see the beauty at her fingertips, and the grace, with which she grows, ahead of her. It was clear that Lauren believed in herself; and that belief was a powerful tool.

We had the opportunity to talk at length about "The Woman I Will Become" which was the journal project of the day. She had a list of grand ideas. And as she listed them off, I realized she purposely did not prioritize them. She listed them as if she was determined to become every one of those things simultaneously.

A Future "I'm Every Woman" was sitting in front of me. I truly saw a young woman who was unafraid to believe in the life of her dreams. I was in awe.

Yes, I remember the first time I saw her. Her eyes were bright; filled with belief. And that image still has a lasting effect on me today.

Abigail Dillon
Professional Artist
Founder of the "I C Beauty Project"

ACKNOWLEDGEMENTS

I wouldn't be where I am today without the support of so many people. If I forgot to list you, please know how important you are to me.

A special thank you to my mom, Tonoa Bond, for teaching me about mindset and making this book come to life. If it weren't for you editing and publishing it, this book wouldn't have existed and would not be a part of my success.

A special thank you to my special teachers from 1st, 2nd, 4th grade, my old choir teacher & my art teacher. Without you many of my academic accomplishments would not have been possible. Thank you for always believing in me no matter what!

To Mrs. Abigail Dillion. Thank you for your "I C Beauty" program and helping me to see the beauty and greatness I hold within. I can now describe in detail "the woman I will become".

To my Nana, thank you for telling other people how amazing you think I am. Our princess tea parties meant the world to me!

To Big Wolf, my brother Brandon. Thank you for giving me advice and life lessons on how to avoid punishments and stay on mom's good side. And for teaching me to be the best Lil' Wolf I can be.

To my auntie Nyce and my cousin Camille. Thank you for supporting me, celebrating me and teaching me awesome things.

Lauren McGowen-Bond

To Jamicia – my photographer, advisor and a great role model. Thank you for the cover photo images, and for always sharing ways I can be great and believing them for me. I definitely look up to you.

To Ms. Vanessa and Mrs. Coleman. Thank you for your support over the years and for seeing great things in me. You and your mom always cheer me on at events as if I am one of the family.

To Ms. Tiffany. Thank you for taking me into your family and celebrating my achievements.

To Tyla. We have shared many platforms, from academic achievements to triathlons. Thank you for always supporting me and for never competing with me. You are truly a great friend.

Thank you to my track and swim coaches for getting me in competition shape. I would not have my medals and ribbons without your help.

A special thanks to those of you who pre-ordered this book before it was done being written. Knowing there were people out there who were willing to support my dreams even before it was complete made me feel accomplished and successful.

And I would like to thank all of my support systems out there who believe in me and always help me to believe in myself!

I would also like to thank YOU! If it were not for you, my book would just be sitting on the shelf. You are a great part of my success and I just want you to know that.

About Lauren

Lauren McGowen-Bond is a 10-year-old mastermind who goes by the name of, "The Dream Mediator." Her life's purpose is to help young people learn to mediate their rough patches so they can believe in and live their biggest dreams. She is an author, speaker, recognized track athlete, triathlete, certified peer mental coach and a trained peer mediator. She is also an audacious influencer who has received numerous academic, artistic and athletic accolades. Two of the most influential: Being inducted into the National Elementary Honor Society, and receiving the President's Award for Educational Excellence. Lauren has written three other books (both non-fiction and fiction) and a motivational song for youth that are currently waiting to be published. She is an avid reader, writer, innovator, film maker, comedian and great friend.

Lauren McGowen-Bond

JOURNAL EXERCISES

Pages 75-89 contain the journal exercises and/or examples of completed exercises for each chapter of this book.

MEDIATION MOMENT:

CONTRACT WITH MYSELF – CHPT. 1

I, _____, hereby commit myself to doing whatever is necessary to believe in myself and my dreams!

I promise myself that no matter what may happen, I will never allow anything to convince me that I cannot have the dreams and things that I am willing to work hard for.

I knowingly accept full responsibility for my own life. I promise to stand fully in my own power and never let anything or anyone take my dreams away from me.

I AM NOT a victim! Therefore, I will hold myself responsible and accountable for my results. And I will always believe in me!

Signed: _____

Date Signed: _____

MEDIATION MOMENT:

YES I CAN – CHPT. 2

Positive self-talk is important for making your dreams come true. This exercise will help you change your mindset from what you believe you cannot do to what you believe you can.

Step 1: Use the "I Believe in Me" journal, or get a piece of paper and title it "YES I CAN!" in **BOLD** ink - Red or any color that stands out.

Step 2: Draw a bunch of random squares around the paper.

Step 3: Think of things that you either cannot do, you're afraid to do or that you want to learn to do.

Step 4: In each square, write the things you thought of in Step 3. (i.e. 'swim', 'ride a bike', 'write a book')

Step 5: It's time to practice! First, begin to chant over and over again, "I Can Do It" while smiling – smiling will help to raise your energy.

Step 6: Next, start chanting the things you wrote in your squares. For example, if you wrote "Swim" in a square, then you will chant: "I Can Do It. I Can Swim.

Step 7: Do this until all the squares are chanted. Remember to keep smiling! And repeat this daily until you believe it!

★★★ YES I CAN! ★★★

Use this page <u>for ideas and a sample</u> of how your board can look.

I CAN RIDE A BIKE!

I CAN CURE CANCER!

I CAN SWIM!

I CAN WRITE A BOOK!

I CAN ACE MY TEST!

I CAN BE A DOCTOR!

I CAN BE NICE TO MY SIBLINGS!

I CAN LOVE MYSELF!

I CAN START AN ORGANIZATION!

I CAN MAKE A DIFFERENCE!

I CAN BELIEVE IN MYSELF!

I CAN STAND UP TO BULLIES!

I CAN CHANGE THE WORLD!

MEDIATION MOMENT:

REDEEMING YOUR POWER – CHPT. 3

When you feel powerless, you have to learn to mediate those feelings. This means, you need to find a way to acknowledge and agree with the power you have inside of you and not allow yourself or your situation to be ***dis***-empowered (or removed from power) as the other person wants you to be.

This exercise will help you feel better and will restore the powerful things you believe about yourself deep down.

Step 1: Use your "I Believe in Me" journal, or get a piece of paper and write down all the mean things a person said to you.

Step 2: Now, tear up this paper and throw the pieces away.

Step 3: Take out a clean sheet of paper and write down good and positive things about yourself.

Step 4: Decorate your paper with whatever makes you feel good.

Step 5: Remember to celebrate yourself and all the good things in you!

REDEEMING YOUR POWER – CHPT. 3
I SEE THE GOOD IN ME!

Using the list below, write down the good and positive things you see in yourself. If you need more space, continue writing on a blank piece of paper. If you cannot think of anything, ask others what they see in you. Write those down and say them to yourself until you can believe them too.

1. _____

2. _____

3. _____

4. _____

5. _____

6. _____

7. _____

8. _____

9. _____

10. _____

11. _____

12. _____

13. _____

14. _____

MEDIATION MOMENT:

EXPECTING GREATNESS – CHPT. 4

My mom taught my classmates and I this exercise when I was in first grade. This exercise involves three questions that once answered will help you to shape your behavior and your expectations so you can have the life you want. The questions will also provide you with the information to help you remember why you should behave a certain way at all times.

In your "I Believe in Me" journal, or on a piece of paper, ask yourself the following questions:

Step 1: "What do I want (to be, to have, or to do)?

Step 2: What proof do I have that what I want is possible or that I can achieve it? (Do I know anyone already doing it?)

Step 3: What am I willing to do right now to have what I want. What behavior(s) am I committing right now that are not moving my dreams forward? Am I willing to change them?

Step 4: Use what you learned about yourself to shape your behaviors. Your behavior shows yourself and the world what you really expect from life. And the only way to get what you expect is to act like it is supposed to come to you. Expect greatness and success and your mind will force you to act in a way to make it come true.

CHOICES FOR CHANGE

*Three Questions to Help Me Make Better
Decisions So I Can Have a Better Life*

---

1. **WHAT DO I WANT** (to be, to have, or to do):

_____

_____

_____

2. **HOW DO I KNOW THAT WHAT I WANT IS
POSSIBLE?** (What evidence or proof do I have that it
can happen?):

_____

_____

_____

3. **WHAT AM I WILLING TO DO RIGHT NOW TO
HAVE WHAT I WANT?:**

_____

_____

_____

MEDIATION MOMENT:

I DARE YOU!!! – CHPT. 5

Daring yourself to try something new is the perfect way to mediate your fears. It allows you to practice feeling the fear but doing it anyway. Below are eight challenges. Have fun! And break out of your comfort zone!

Step 1: Perform a dare from the list below. Then, write down what you learned about yourself after each dare was completed. And if you need to, do them again and again.

DARE #1: Eat something you've been afraid to try before.
DARE #2: Give three strangers, close to your age, a high-five and shout, "Hey, what's up!"
DARE #3: For 21 days, look yourself in the mirror for at least one minute and say, "I Love You!" Keep track of each day.
DARE #4: Find a friend being bullied and sit w/them for lunch or recess or walk with them down the hall.
DARE #5: Write a letter to someone and tell them they are awesome (stranger, friend, person you don't like, etc.).
DARE #6: Make encouraging notecards and pass them out to bullies. ("You are awesome… you are important", etc.)
DARE #7: Find someone younger than you to encourage and for two weeks call them, visit them, or walk them to school.
-------BONUS-------
DARE #8: Dance wildly in public while shouting, "I'm a little pony."

I DARE YOU CHALLENGES
• WHAT I LEARNED ABOUT ME •

✳ **DARE #1**:

_____

✳ **DARE #2**:

_____

✳ **DARE #3**:

_____

✳ **DARE #4**:

_____

✳ **DARE #5**:

_____

✳ **DARE #6**:

_____

✳ **DARE #7**:

_____

✳ **DARE #8**:

_____

MEDIATION MOMENT:

I AM POSSIBLE – CHPT. 6

The words "I AM" are two of the most powerful words in the Universe because what follows them the mind automatically believes. The brain can only see in others what it already recognizes in itself. Doing this exercise, you will use others as your guide to bring the best things about yourself that are hidden to the light. And once you see it, you will have no choice but to believe it and then live it!

Step 1: Using the "I Believe in Me" journal, or a piece of paper, draw a line to divide the paper down the middle.

Step 2: Think of three people you admire. On the left side of the paper, on each line, write the reasons you admire them.

Step 3: On the right side, next to what you wrote you are going to write "I AM" followed by the opposite of what you wrote in the left column. So, if you wrote "honest" in the left column then in the right hand column, on the same line but next to it, you are going to write, "I AM Honest!"

Step 4: After you have written down as many opposites as you want, you will then fold the paper in half until you only see the right hand column.

Step 5: **MIRROR TIME**: Every day and night, for at least 21 days, practice these in the mirror until you believe them.

I AM! EXERCISE

Because I AM Worth It!

TRAITS OF SOMEONE I ADMIRE	WRITE "I AM... (INSERT TRAIT)"
(Example: Smart) *(Example: Fearless)*	*(Example: I AM Smart)* *(Example: I AM Fearless)*

MEDIATION MOMENT:

ADVOCATING FOR YOUR DREAMS – CHPT. 7

This mediation will include a list of options as there are many ways to advocate for yourself. The key is to find the most authentic one that represents you and fits with your situation.

Option 1:
1. Create a list of people you can ask for support from. Include the type of support you can receive from them. Now, you have a master list for whenever you need it.

Option 2:
1. Create a mirror. Find someone or a group of people who are either living the life you would like to live or whose life you would like to mirror. Write down all the traits or things about them that you would like to mirror. Leave space so that when you accomplish those things, or something like it, you can keep track. Consider this (healthy) competition from afar. They never even have to know – unless you want them to.

Option 1:
1. Find pictures of high achieving people that you admire. They can be celebrities, scientists, politicians, family, whomever.
2. Tape their pictures to a poster board to look at, whenever you're having problems believing in yourself, as a reminder of what is possible. Remember, if one person can do it, you can too!

◀) MY BIGGEST SUPPORTERS ◀)

WHO WILL SUPPORT ME & HOW	PEOPLE I CAN MIRROR
(Example: My Mom) (She will motivate me to do my best)	*(Example: Lauren because she believes in her dreams)*

MEDIATION MOMENT #8A:

EX #1: DREAMING W/YOUR EYES OPEN – CHPT. 8

Dreaming with your eyes open requires you to form your identity. You have to believe in yourself and believe your dreams can come true. Let's create a dream/identity board!

Step 1: On pieces of paper cut into squares or circles, write down what you want in life. It's okay for these to be either material things, things that apply to your legacy, or whatever you want to be known for when you leave this earth. For instance, if you want to be a doctor, you would write "Be a Doctor". If you want to travel the world, you would write "Travel". If it is to drive a certain car, you would simply write, the name of the car.

Step 2: Get a poster board. In random patterns, use tape, staples, or push pins to attach your words to the board.

Step 3: Next, using magazines, newspapers, or the internet, cut out images that match what you wrote and put them on the board next to the word.

Step 4: Every day, week or month, continue to add to your board with any new dreams.

Step 5: Look at your board every day and always believe your dreams are possible!

MEDIATION MOMENT #8B:

EX #2: THE CALM WITHIN THE STORM – CHPT. 8

Sometimes when your dreams are really big you freak out a little bit, right? Calming jars are SO COOL! Shaking the jar and watching the glitter settle will help you to calm any fears you have relating to your dreams so that you remember to say, "I AM POSSIBLE!"

For this you will need:

• Hot Water	• Clear School Glue (It has to be clear not white)
• Glitter (Favorite colors)	• Food Coloring (Optional)
•A New or Recycled Bottle (glass or plastic). Ex: Water or Juice Bottle, Relish Jar, etc.	• Funnel (Optional) • Strong Glue or Duct Tape

Directions (Young kids please get your parent's to help you):
1. Fill bottle ¾ full with hot water
2. Add entire bottle of clear glue to thicken the water
3. Add glitter. As much or as little for the look you want
4. Add one tiny drop of food coloring to enhance color
5. Stir – Stir – Stir
6. For fun, add toys, sequins, beads, shells, jewels, etc.
7. When mixed how you want, glue or tape lid to the bottle
8. Shake and enjoy!

(Go to www.ToKnowaDream.com for video tutorial)

 **RESOURCES**

••

For samples of the exercises mentioned in the book as well as other mediation coaching and motivational tips, go to www.ToKnowADream.com/BelieveBook. Click the link for book freebies. Enter the password - FREEBELIEFTOOLS

SOURCE CREDIT

Credit For Sources Used in the Book Are As Follows:

THE BELIEVER'S CREED – Adapted from the poem "The Learner's Creed written by: Ernestine Stewart Mitchell

Choices for Change Exercise. Created by, Tonoa Bond. For To Know a Dream International.

All quotes used in the book fall under the guidelines of fair use permission

WORK WITH LAUREN

Helping teens & youth reach for their dreams

To Know a Dream International
Where we believe, no age is too young to
begin your dreams.

ONLINE WORKSHOPS ★ GROUP COACHING PROGRAMS
CELEBRITY INTERVIEWS ★ MEDIATION TECHNIQUES ★
EMAIL SUPPORT GROUPS ★ MOTIVATIONAL VIDEOS ★
VISION BOARD PARTIES ★ SLEEPOVER CAMPS ★ DREAM
EXPLOSION CONFERENCES ★ ...AND MORE ★

LAUREN HAS A MASTERMIND THAT IS SPECIFICALLY FOR YOU.

Become a part of Lauren's Elite Inner Circle. Here you will learn to use some of Lauren's tried and true techniques for believing in herself, and you will watch your confidence, your beliefs and your dreams EXPLODE!!!

Join Today! Because trust me... Lauren's Inner Circle will not be the same without you! ❤ 💙 ❤ 💙

Investment of $9.97mo

www.ToKnowADream.com (Lauren's Inner Circle)

Price includes a monthly call with Lauren, special monthly video message, affirmation print outs for your vision boards... & more.

*Under 18? Must have your parent's permission. Sorry, but it's the law!

WANT TO WRITE A BOOK

Join AIM High Media & Publishing's Virtual Youth Writing Workshops.

AIM High Media & Publishing offers great packages for emerging youth authors to help them offer their voices to the world.

Our private 6-week intensives are individually designed lessons and curriculum for student's interests and passion.

Our workshops nourish the gifts of youth by showing them a mirror of their own abilities.

Through fun yet intensive private lessons, we teach the art of writing while coaching and empowering youth to never give up on their dreams.

Student's will leave this workshop ready to become a published author. Depending on their writing speed, they will either have an idea, an expanded outline, or a book ready for electronic print (Kindle, iBooks, Nook or eBook). Some packages include ISBN and Library of Congress Control Numbers).

Visit AIMHighPub.com for more information.